Also by PIET HEIN

GROOKS 1
GROOKS 3

GROOKS
2

PIET HEIN

GROOKS

2

GENERAL PUBLISHING COMPANY LIMITED
TORONTO

With the assistance of Jens Arup

General Publishing Company Limited
30 Lesmill Road
DON MILLS, Ontario

First Canadian Edition
Reprinted 1970, 1971

The collections of
GROOKS
are published by
General Publishing Co. Ltd
Ontario, Canada
Doubleday & Company, Inc.
New York, U.S.A.
Hodder and Stoughton Limited
London, England
and
BORGENS FORLAG
Copenhagen, Denmark

Over 310,000 copies of GROOKS
printed in English
62,000 copies in print in Canada

ISBN 0-7736-1003-0 (paperback)
ISBN 0-7736-0012-4 (hardcover)

Printed in Canada by
T. H. Best Printing Company Limited

TO
CHARLES CHAPLIN

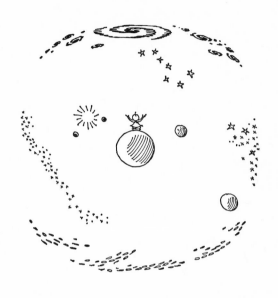

NOTHING IS INDISPENSABLE

Grook to warn the universe against megalomania

> The universe may
> be as great as they say.
> But it wouldn't be missed
> if it didn't exist.

TIME AND ETERNITY

Where the woods and ploughlands
of tradition and modernity
run into the never-ending
deserts of eternity,
there I have my daily task,
while time smoothly passes,
spooning the eternal sands
into hour-glasses.

INVESTMENT POLICY

Anxieties yield
at a negative rate,
increasing in smallness
the longer they wait.

A WORD OF ENCOURAGEMENT

Stomach-ache can be a curse;
heart-ache may be even worse;
so thank Heaven on your knees
if you've got but one of these.

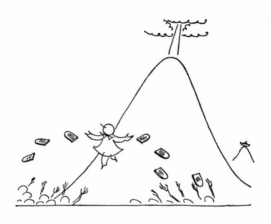

LARGESSE

A grook about giving of one's plenty

It's pleasant to give
    without feeling the price;
so let us be
    nobly profuse of
the bottomless treasure
    of moral advice
we anyhow
    never make use of.

ALLOTMENT

Your days on earth
are just so few
that there's exactly
time to do
the things that don't
appeal to you.

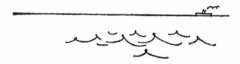

THE FINAL STEP

Motto: Il n'y a que le
dernier pas qui coûte.

If they made diving boards
    six inches shorter -
think how much sooner
    you'd be in the water.

THOUGHTS
ON A STATION PLATFORM

It ought to be plain
how little you gain
by getting excited
   and vexed.
You'll always be late
for the previous train,
and always in time
   for the next.

AN OLD SAW RESET

To keep an
ever-open door
is wisdom's true advancer;
so they are fools
who don't ask more
than ten wise men can answer.

THE UNTENABLE ARGUMENT

My adversary's argument
is not alone malevolent
    but ignorant to boot.
He hasn't even got the sense
to state his so-called evidence
    in terms I can refute.

THE WISDOM OF THE SPHERES

How instructive
    is a star!
It can teach us
    from afar
just how small
    each other are.

IT ISN'T ENOUGH

One paramount truth
our society smothers
in petty concern
with position and pelf:
It isn't enough
to exasperate others;
you've got to remember
to gladden yourself.

WHAT LOVE IS LIKE

Love is like
a pineapple,
sweet and
undefinable.

THE GRASSHOPPER'S GRIEF

A fable

A grasshopper sat on a flagstone and wept
    with a sorrow that few surpass.
He had painfully mastered his letters, and leapt
to a place where he knew an inscription was kept;
    and of course it said:
        KEEP OFF THE GRASS

SMALL THINGS AND GREAT

He that lets
the small things bind him
leaves the great
undone behind him.

BRAVE

To be brave is to behave
bravely when your heart is faint.
So you can be really brave
only when you really ain't.

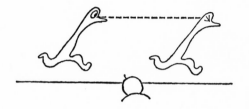

ABREAST

He who aims
to keep abreast
is for ever
second best.

ENOUGH

is more than enough

Of drink
and victuals
and suchlike
stuff
a bit
too little
is just
enough.

THE STATE

Nature, our father and mother,
gave us all we have got.
The state, our elder brother,
swipes the lot.

POW!

That baddies are baddies
    is only too true,
however one studies
    the things that they do.
But what I find sad is
    how painfully few
have noticed that goodies
    are too.

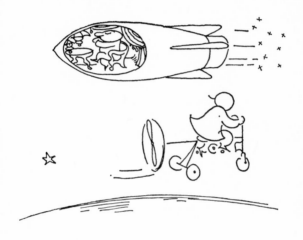

PRESENCE OF MIND

You'll conquer the present
    suspiciously fast
if you smell of the future
    —and stink of the past.

THE SLOT MACHINE

A contribution to the psychology of disappointment

Yes, life is a gamble;
but isn't it mean
that you're never the one
to win it,
when the thing is
a coin-in-the-slot machine,
and you did
put a shirt-button in it.

TIMING TOAST

Grook on how to char for yourself

There's an art of knowing when.
Never try to guess.
Toast until it smokes and then
twenty seconds less.

AN ECHO FROM THE PAST

Exercise for military minds

Prehistoric monsters straying
    on a Wellsian rampage?
Martian saucerers surveying
    their terrestrial landing stage?
Say, what is that hideous braying,
    eloquent of fear and rage?
Only Homo sapiens, playing
    at the pre-atomic age.

FREEDOM

Freedom means
you're free to do
just whatever
pleases you;
- if, of course
that is to say,
what you please
is what you may.

THE ARITHMETIC OF CO-OPERATION

When you're adding up committees
there's a useful rule of thumb:
that talents make a difference,
but follies make a sum.

CONSTITUTIONAL POINT

Power corrupts,
whereas sound opposition
builds up our free
democratic tradition.
One thing would make
a democracy flower:
having a strong opposition -
in power.

THE OVERDOERS

Truth shall emerge from the interplay
    of attitudes freely debated.
Don't be misled by fanatics who say
    that only one truth should be stated:
truth is constructed in such a way
    that it can't be exaggerated.

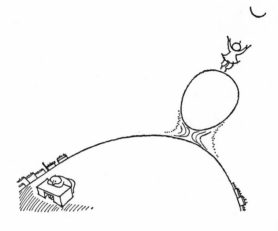

MAKING AN EFFORT

Our so-called limitations, I believe,
apply to faculties we don't apply.
We don't discover what we can't achieve
until we make an effort not to try.

RHYME AND REASON

There was an old woman
who lived in a shoe.
She had so many children.
She didn't know what to do.
But try as she would
she could never detect
which was the cause
and which the effect.

WHAT PEOPLE MAY THINK

Some people cower
    and wince and shrink,
owing to fear of
    what people may think.
There is one answer
    to worries like these:
people may think
    what the devil they please.

THE ONLY SOLUTION

We shall have to evolve
problem-solvers galore -
since each problem they solve
creates ten problems more.

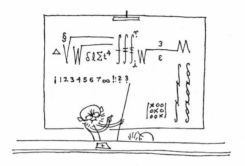

WIDE ROAD

To make a name for learning
when other roads are barred,
take something very easy
and make it very hard.

WHEN IGNORANTS-

We're leaving WISDOM
    to starve and thirst
when we cultivate
    KNOWLEDGE as such.
The very best comes
    to the very worst
WHEN IGNORANTS
    KNOW TOO MUCH.

DEAD REASONABLE

>> ... that reason died
last night at eleven.<<
Henrik Ibsen: >>Peer Gynt<<

Somebody said
that Reason was dead.
Reason said: No,
I think not so.

REFLECTION ON SIZE

Small people often overrate
the charm of being tall;
which is, that you appreciate
the charm of being small.

A REPROOF

Grook in answer to a long explanatory letter

In view of your manner
    of spending your days
I hope you may learn,
    before ending them,
that the effort you spend
    on defending your ways
could better be spent
    on amending them.

THE FINAL TOUCH

Portrait of nobody in particular

Idiots are really
one hundred per cent
when they are also
intelligent.

THE GIOCONDA SIMILE

Certainly Leonardo's
magical Mona Lisa
may be superbly rendered
    using a dozen tiles.
Such things are not unusual.
Yet there are those who always
feel that there's something subtle
    gone from the way she smiles.

THAT'S WHY

Why do bad writers
    win the fight?
Why do good writers
    die in need?
Because the writers
    who can't write
are read by readers
    who can't read.

STONE IN SHOE

If a nasty jagged stone
gets into your shoe,
thank the Lord it came alone —
what if it were two?

LIKE A TALL, SOLID BEECH TREE

Spring grook

I'm sitting with my back against
        a tall, solid beech tree,
feeling time flowing
        in a strong, cool stream,
feeling life rising
        like a tall, solid beech tree
emerging from Eternity's
        unending dream.

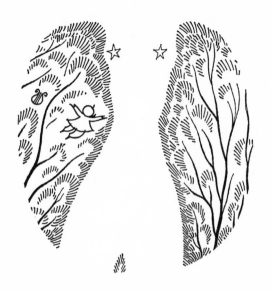

MEMENTO VIVERE

Love while you've got
love to give.
Live while you've got
life to live.

THE UNATTAINABLE IDEAL

We ought to live
    each day as though
it were our last day
    here below.

But if I did, alas,
    I know
it would have killed me
    long ago.

MEAN VALUE

We hope our share of luck will come
to some unlikely maximum.

We fear, when nightmare fears benumb,
a catastrophic minimum.

But nonetheless the final sum
is Nature's well-known middlemum.

GOOD ADVICE

Shun advice
at any price -
that's what I call
good advice.

THE ME ABOVE THE ME

Giving in is no defeat.
Passing on is no retreat.
Selves are made to rise above.
You shall live in what you love.

SUB SPECIE -

Sub specie
aeternitatis
even the dearest bought
is gratis.

WHO AM I?

Who am I
to deny
that maybe
God is me?

THE ULTIMATE WISDOM

Philosophers
must ultimately find
their true perfection

in knowing all
the follies of mankind
- by introspection.

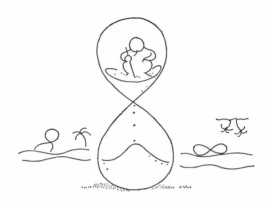

FORM AND MATERIAL

A grook about the impermanence of language

I see myself and what I write enclosed in
an hour-glass's uppermost retort.
The very stuff my patterns are composed in
must fall away, and crumble down to naught.

Yet stubbornly, and in despite of reason,
I still believe that what is fashioned there
will, when the sands run out in destined season,
remain unchanged, suspended in the air.

A TIP

to members of the literary profession

Those
who can write
have a
    lot to
learn from those
bright
enough
    not to.

ADVICE AT NIGHTFALL

Smile
a while
ere day
    is done
and all
your gall
will soon
    be gone.

TITLE INDEX

First line index